COMMUNITY · CONNECTIONS

?

WHAT DOES IT DO?
CRANE

BY JOSH GREGORY

Published in the United States of America by Cherry Lake Publishing
Ann Arbor, Michigan
www.cherrylakepublishing.com

Content Adviser: Louis Teel, Professor of Heavy Equipment, Central Arizona College
Reading Adviser: Cecilia Minden-Cupp, PhD, Literacy Consultant

Photo Credits: Cover and page 1, ©iStockphoto.com/vkyryl; page 5, ©Stephen Finn/
Shutterstock, Inc.; page 7, ©iStockphoto.com/ftwitty; page 9, ©Lilia Barladyan/Shutterstock,
Inc.; page 11, ©Fernando Cortes/Shutterstock, Inc.; page 13, ©Mtrebbin/Shutterstock, Inc.;
page 15, ©Jurand/Shutterstock, Inc.; page 17, ©iStockphoto.com/Lya_Cattel; page 19,
©Antikainen/Shutterstock, Inc.; page 21, ©iStockphoto.com/rhyman007

LIBRARY OF CONGRESS CATALOGING-IN-PUBLICATION DATA
Gregory, Josh.
  What does it do? Crane/by Josh Gregory.
    p. cm.—(Community connections)
  Includes bibliographical references and index.
  ISBN-13: 978-1-60279-967-7 (lib. bdg.)
  ISBN-10: 1-60279-967-9 (lib. bdg.)
  1. Cranes—Juvenile literature. I. Title. II. Title: Crane. III. Series.
  TJ1363.G785 2010
  621.8'73—dc22   2010023582

Cherry Lake Publishing would like to acknowledge the
work of The Partnership for 21st Century Skills. Please
visit www.21stcenturyskills.org for more information.

Printed in the United States of America
Corporate Graphics Inc.
January 2011
CLSP08

CONTENTS

WHAT DOES IT DO?

HOW DID THEY GET THAT UP THERE?

You look out the school bus window. People are hard at work on a building.

Right now, the building is nothing more than a frame. Soon, it will have walls and windows. It will be a tall building. How will the **building materials** get up that high?

It takes a lot of work to put up a tall building.

Cranes are special machines that lift things up high. They move things that are big or heavy.

How do workers connect cranes to the objects they want to move? They use hooks, **magnets**, or buckets. Then the cranes can lift the objects up. They can also move the objects from side to side.

Workers often use hooks and strong cables to connect things to cranes.

TOWER CRANES

There are many different types of cranes. Each type is best for a certain kind of job.

Tower cranes are great for building skyscrapers and other tall buildings. They can reach 150 feet (45.7 meters) or more into the air. They can lift up to 19 tons.

More than one tower crane may be needed to build a big skyscraper!

The base of a tower crane is bolted to a **concrete** pad. This keeps the crane from falling over.

A tall tower rises up from the base. Workers can make this tower taller.

There is a small box at the top of the tower. This is where the crane **operator** sits.

The operator sits in a box near the top of a crane's tower.

11

A tower crane has a long arm called a **jib**. It sticks out from the tower. A **trolley** runs along the jib. A **cable** with a hook hangs from the trolley.

The cable winds up to lift things. Operators can move the trolley back and forth. They can also spin the jib around. This moves things from side to side.

The trolley and jib help the crane operator move things.

Weights are added to one end of the jib before lifting anything. Why? Think about a teeter-totter. What happens when only one person sits on a teeter-totter? Now think about a tower crane. What would happen if there were no weights on the jib?

13

OTHER KINDS OF CRANES

Big ships carry goods around the world. Some goods are packed into **containers**. The containers are large and heavy.

Container cranes load the containers onto ships. They also unload the ships.

You will find many cranes at a shipping dock.

Sometimes, workers need cranes that move easily from place to place. Truck cranes are perfect for these jobs.

A truck crane is a heavy truck with a crane built into the back. Workers run the crane using controls on the truck. These cranes cannot lift as much as other kinds of cranes. Too much weight would tip them over!

Truck cranes can be used in spaces too small for tower cranes.

Which jobs are best for truck cranes? Think about tower cranes. They take up a lot of space. Tower cranes must be built before workers can use them. This is a lot of work. When would a truck crane be a better choice?

17

A bridge crane is another type of crane. Cables hang from a trolley. The trolley runs along a beam called a bridge. The trolley can move from side to side. The bridge can also move back and forth.

Bridge cranes can reach all around a large room. They are used in big warehouses.

Bridge cranes are used in factories and warehouses.

Qт 32т

Qт=17,5т

Qт=17,5т

19

Look closely the next time you pass a job site. Do you see a tower crane? How about a truck crane?

Now you know how workers can put up such tall buildings! Aren't cranes helpful machines?

How many cranes do you see in this picture?

Think about the places where cranes are used. Do you have any friends or family members who work at those places? Ask them about ways that cranes help get work done. You might be surprised by what you learn!

21

GLOSSARY

building materials (BIL-ding muh-TIHR-ee-uhlz) things used to build, such as bricks and lumber

cable (KAY-buhl) a strong metal rope

concrete (KON-kreet) a special mix of sand, cement, water, and tiny stones

containers (kuhn-TAYN-erz) boxes that hold goods and are loaded onto ships

jib (JIB) the arm of a crane

magnets (MAG-nitss) objects that pull things made of iron or steel toward themselves

operator (OP-uh-ray-tur) a person who controls the movements of a crane

trolley (TROL-ee) a cart that runs along rails

FIND OUT MORE

BOOKS

Becker, Ann. *Cranes.* New York: Marshall Cavendish Benchmark, 2010.

Tourville, Amanda Doering. *Cranes.* Edina, MN: Magic Wagon, 2009.

WEB SITES

PBS—Building Big: Skyscrapers
www.pbs.org/wgbh/buildingbig/skyscraper/index.html
Visit this site to learn more about skyscrapers.

TLC—How to Draw Cranes in 10 Steps
tlc.howstuffworks.com/family/how-to-draw-cranes1.htm
Find out more about cranes as you learn how to draw one.

INDEX

ABOUT THE AUTHOR

Josh Gregory writes and edits books for kids. He lives in Chicago, Illinois.